The Home-Based Daycare Owner

I0446765

Starting and Running a Safe and
Profitable Childcare Business

Introduction

In the very heart of every community, there lies a hidden gem that simultaneously functions as a sanctuary for young minds, a lifeline for busy parents, and an embodiment of entrepreneurial spirit - a home-based daycare. This book, "The Home-Based Daycare Owner: Starting and Running a Safe and Profitable Childcare Business," is meticulously crafted for those looking to embark on the captivating journey of opening and operating a successful home-based daycare.

The world of a home-based childcare service is one of exciting opportunities and rewarding experiences, intertwined with the promise of a sustainable and profitable venture. It is an intricately woven tapestry of creativity, responsibility, and business acumen. This book serves as the perfect guide, shining light on how to effectively navigate this complex, yet wonderfully fulfilling, endeavor.

From understanding the daycare business model, through to implementing health and safety guidelines, and fostering relationships with customers, this book covers the entire spectrum of running a successful daycare business out of the comfort of your home. Its pages are packed with the vital knowledge needed to create a safe, nurturing, and engaging environment for children, while also ensuring you have a robust business model that consents profitability and growth.

Whether you have a knack for nurturing young minds, a drive to contribute positively to your community, or you are merely in search of a fitting entrepreneurial expedition, "The Home-Based Daycare Owner" provides you with a beacon to guide you on this significant journey. This book, with its practical insights, real tips, and proven strategies, stands ready to accompany you on your quest to start and run not just a daycare, but a thriving community of young learners, dedicated parents, and successful entrepreneurs.

Welcome to a world where nurturing young minds and nurturing a successful business coexist, where the laughter of children echoes against the backdrop of entrepreneurial achievement. Welcome to the world of home-based daycare!

Chapter One

Introduction to Home-Based Daycare

1.1 What is Home-Based Daycare?

Home-based daycare, often referred to as family childcare or in-home daycare, constitutes a rapidly growing and increasingly popular sector of the childcare industry. It involves the provision of childcare services in the friendly confines of an entrepreneur's residence. This model of childcare offers a unique blend of love, comfort, and professionalism, creating a hospitable learning environment that caters to the needs of children and their families.

Personalized, Family-Oriented Environment

One striking feature of a home-based daycare is the remarkably personalized and family-oriented ambience it boasts. Unlike large commercial childcare centres, an in-home daycare can accommodate a smaller group of children, thereby allowing for one-on-one attention, fostering strong relationships, and ultimately providing a customized experience for each child. This personalized approach helps to create a warm and secure atmosphere akin to a child's own home, which is especially valuable for young kids who might struggle with unfamiliar environments.

Flexibility and Versatility

Operating a home-based daycare offers unparalleled flexibility and versatility. With the capacity to establish your policies, routines, and approaches to childcare, you have the liberty to design a program that aligns with your own values, goals, and educational philosophies. This flexibility also extends to parents who may benefit from varied hours of operation and additional services that may not be readily available at larger childcare facilities.

Diverse Ages and Abilities

A noteworthy characteristic of home-based daycares is their proficiency in catering to an extensive range of ages and abilities. They often simultaneously accommodate infants, toddlers, preschoolers, and school-aged children. This diversity not only allows siblings to attend the same daycare but also generates opportunities for younger and older children to interact and learn from one another. By encountering peers with varied skills, interests, and learning styles, children in home-based daycares are introduced to a wealth of new experiences and valuable life lessons.

Optimal Child-to-Caregiver Ratio

A distinctive benefit of home-based daycares is the relatively low child-to-caregiver ratio - a crucial determinant of quality childcare. Small groups ensure that children receive appropriate attention, enabling caregivers to create strong bonds with kids and responding to their individual needs and preferences more effectively. This personal connection can lead to enhanced emotional development and improved well-being for children, as well as a better understanding of each child's unique developmental journey.

Cost Effectiveness

For both the provider and the client, home-based daycares present a cost-effective option when compared to larger childcare centres. Running a daycare from one's home enables entrepreneurs to reduce overhead costs and, in turn, offers more affordable childcare to families.

Budget-conscious parents often appreciate the lower fees often associated with in-home daycares, without having to compromise on the quality of care their children receive.

1.2 Why Choose a Career in Home-Based Daycare?

A career in home-based daycare presents countless opportunities for both personal and professional growth, alongside the immense satisfaction of nurturing young minds and fostering a sense of community. Choosing a career in this field opens the doors for making a tangible and lasting impact on the lives of children and families while tapping into several advantages that may not be available in other career paths. Here are a few compelling reasons why you should consider a career in home-based daycare:

Personal Fulfillment and Emotional Rewards

Being directly involved in the intellectual, social, and emotional development of children can be an incredibly fulfilling experience. As a home-based daycare provider, you have the freedom to create a nurturing environment and help shape the minds of future generations. Witnessing the growth, progress, and individual achievements of each child who passes through your doors brings unbridled joy and a deep satisfaction that few other careers can provide.

Entrepreneurial Independence and Creativity

Home-based daycare provides the perfect opportunity to unleash your entrepreneurial spirit and creativity. By designing your child-centred curriculum, daily routines, and policies, you can create a unique experience that showcases your passion for childcare, educational philosophy, and personal values. The opportunity to take full control of establishing and managing a successful business while positively impacting the lives of children and their families is priceless.

Flexibility and Work-Life Balance

Operating a daycare service from your home allows you to establish a favourable work-life balance, even as you pursue your passion for childcare. With the autonomy to set your hours of operation, and the convenience of working from home, you have more time and energy to invest in personal pursuits and family commitments. Additionally, for entrepreneurs with their own young children, this arrangement presents a wonderful opportunity to spend precious time with them while pursuing a successful career in childcare.

Financial Benefits and Opportunities

A home-based daycare business is not only emotionally rewarding but can also lead to financial success. By offering childcare services from your home, you can significantly reduce overhead costs and maximize profitability. Furthermore, the sustained demand for quality childcare ensures that your business remains viable and lucrative, providing you with steady income and growth opportunities as you cater to your community's childcare needs.

Building Strong Relationships and Community Connections

Choosing a career in home-based daycare enables you to build strong, long-lasting relationships with children, families, and your community at large. By creating an inclusive and welcoming atmosphere, you will foster a sense of camaraderie and support among your clients.

These connections often transcend the limits of your daycare services, creating a network of people who share common values, goals, and appreciation for the importance of nurturing young minds. This enriching network strengthens your business and helps solidify your role as a prominent contributor to your community.

Chapter two

Understanding the Daycare Business Model

2.1 The Basic Childcare Business Model

Diving into the home-based daycare business requires a comprehension of the fundamental childcare business model that underpins successful operations. A well-constructed business model sets the groundwork for efficient management, sustainable growth, and profitability in any daycare setting, including the home-based environment. Here are the key components to help you understand the basic childcare business model for a home-based daycare owner:

Market Research and Target Clientele

Taking the time to conduct thorough market research is essential for understanding the local childcare landscape, competition, and most importantly, the demand for childcare services in your area. Assessing the needs of your target clientele—families with young children—will enable you to tailor your services to meet their requirements. Consider factors like the age group you want to focus on, flexible hours, and additional offerings that may appeal to your potential clients, such as early drop-off and late pick-up options.

Fee Structure and Revenue Streams

A vital aspect of the childcare business model is determining an appropriate fee structure for your home-based daycare. This includes deciding on competitive pricing, payment policies, and discounts, if applicable, such as sibling discounts, or reduced rates for full-time enrollees. Additional revenue streams can also be incorporated to boost profitability, including offering extra services like art classes, music or dance classes, and childcare during holidays or off-peak hours.

Costs and Expenses

Thoroughly understanding and managing costs and expenses lie at the heart of a profitable home-based daycare business. Consider fixed costs such as rent or mortgage payments, utilities, licensing fees, insurance, and maintenance, and variable costs like food, supplies, educational materials, and staff wages, if applicable. Planning and organizing these expenses is crucial for sustaining the financial health of your business.

Licensing and Regulations

Adhering to local and regional licensing requirements, as well as regulations for child-to-caregiver ratios, health and safety, and staff qualifications, is a fundamental component of any successful daycare business. Ensuring compliance not only safeguards your business from potential legal issues but also instils confidence in your clients and demonstrates your commitment to providing a secure and supportive environment for their children.

Curriculum and Daily Activities

A well-designed and age-appropriate curriculum is the backbone of a thriving daycare business. Planning and implementing daily activities that encompass learning objectives, while incorporating elements of play and creativity, is essential. Structured activities, including art, music, and movement, combined with ample opportunities for free play and self-directed exploration fosters a stimulating and nurturing environment that resonates with both children and parents.

Marketing and Community Outreach

Promoting your home-based daycare and building a strong community presence is vital for business success. This includes online and offline marketing efforts, such as maintaining a user-friendly website, actively engaging on social media, participating in local events, and networking with other childcare and education professionals. Establishing a positive reputation within your community will have a direct impact on enrollment numbers, client satisfaction, and word-of-mouth referrals.

Continuous Improvement and Adaptability

A successful home-based daycare business model embraces continuous improvement and adaptability. Regularly evaluate your operations, seek feedback from clients, gather insights and inspiration from new educational theories, and stay informed about the latest industry trends. This growth-focused mindset will enable you to refine your business offerings, improve client satisfaction, and remain competitive within your market.

2.2 Challenges in Home-Based Daycare

While a home-based daycare business can be rewarding, there are also several challenges associated with it that should be factored into the overall business model. Understanding these challenges can help budding entrepreneurs strategize effectively, plan for contingencies, and foster a more resilient daycare business. This section aims to elaborate on some of these potential challenges to help deepen your understanding of the business model of home-based daycare.

Licensing and Regulatory Standards

One of the primary challenges home-based daycare providers grapple with is complying with local and regional licensing and regulatory standards. This process can be time-consuming and complex, requiring a thorough understanding of safety protocols, child-to-caretaker ratios, facility specifications, and other applicable regulations. Non-compliance can result in penalties and harm the reputation of the daycare, so it's crucial to stay updated on any changes in standards or requirements.

Balancing Work and Home Life

Managing a daycare from home blurs the line between personal and professional life, which can lead to difficulties in achieving a comfortable work-life balance. Challenges may include finding alone time, creating boundaries between work and leisure spaces, and balancing the demands of childcare with household chores and other personal commitments. Successful home-based daycare owners often need to develop strong time-management skills and routines to overcome this issue.

Financial Sustainability

Maintaining financial sustainability amid variable enrollment numbers and operating costs can be a daunting task. Factors such as seasonal fluctuations in enrollment, competition from other daycare services, and unforeseen expenses can impact profitability. Effective financial planning and budgeting, including the exploration of alternative revenue streams, are crucial for managing this challenge.

Sourcing Reliable and Cost-Effective Supplies

Daycare providers need a continuous supply of various materials, including educational supplies, arts and crafts, snacks, and more. Finding reliable and cost-effective sources for these supplies can be a challenge, particularly for new businesses. Careful research, fostering strong vendor relationships, and bulk purchasing are potential strategies to navigate this challenge.

Constant Vigilance and High Levels of Energy

Working with young children requires constant vigilance and high levels of energy. Since injuries can occur with little notice, providers must always keep a watchful eye on the children. Additionally, running an engaging, interactive daycare requires a great deal of physical and mental energy. It's important to incorporate breaks and self-care habits into the daily routine to avoid burnout.

Marketing and Enrollment

Attracting and retaining clients in a competitive market can be a significant challenge. Effective marketing, offering unique services, establishing a positive reputation, and forming strong relationships with families are all vital components of a successful enrollment strategy. Balancing the need for maximum enrollment with the necessity of maintaining a manageable child-to-caregiver ratio can also require careful planning and adaptability.

2.3 Competition Assessment

Evaluating competition is an integral aspect of creating a viable business model for a home-based daycare. Without understanding the strengths, weaknesses, and unique offerings of your competition, it would be nearly impossible to identify gaps in the market or set yourself apart. A thorough competition assessment can provide valuable insights that help refine and enhance your own home-based daycare operation.

Understanding Your Competition

Firstly, identifying your direct and indirect competition is necessary. Direct competition includes other home-based daycares in your area, while indirect competition can be commercial daycare centres, pre-schools, or even babysitters and nannies. Conduct comprehensive research into how they operate, what services they offer, their fee structure, how they market themselves, their operating hours, and unique selling points.

Analysing Strengths and Weaknesses

Analyze your competitors' strengths and weaknesses. This can be done through various methods such as visiting their websites, and social media platforms, attending open houses, or reading reviews posted by parents. Understanding what they do well can provide guidance on what your target market values. At the same time, pinpointing their weaknesses can highlight potential opportunities for your daycare business.

Scoping Out Unique Services

Part of the competitive assessment includes identifying unique services that competitors offer which make them stand out. These might include extended hours of operation, an impressive curriculum, specific teaching philosophies, offering meals or transportation, extra-curricular activities, or state-of-the-art facilities. These unique services can be a deciding factor for parents when choosing a daycare.

Assessing Fee Structures and Affordability

Examining the fee structures of your competition is pivotal. Understand if their rates are hourly, daily, weekly, or monthly and what services are included within these fees. This can provide a baseline when deciding your own pricing strategy while still ensuring affordability for your clients.

Evaluating Marketing Strategies

You can learn a lot from your competitors' marketing strategies. Are they active on social media? Do they have a well-designed website? Do they host community events? Do they rely on word-of-mouth referrals? Understanding these strategies will give you a better idea of what resonates with your target market and which avenues might be worth exploring to attract potential clients.

Identifying Areas of Opportunity

Finally, assess areas of opportunity within your local daycare market. This might involve offering services or conveniences that local competitors aren't currently providing or simply doing a better job in areas where competitors are lagging. This could be as simple as longer operating hours, or as involved as a specialized curriculum. Identifying what the parents in your area need and want from childcare, but can't get from existing providers, is key to your success.

Chapter three

Requirements for Starting a Home-Based Daycare

3.1 Legal Requirements

Starting a home-based daycare is not just about setting up a nurturing environment for children. It also necessitates comprehending and complying with various legal requirements. These laws and regulations, which differ widely based on location, are designed to ensure the safety and well-being of the children in your care. While the specifics differ from place to place, here are general areas to familiarize yourself with when setting up your home-based daycare:

Business Licensing

Most jurisdictions require daycare providers to obtain a business license. The process typically involves submitting a detailed application, sometimes including a business plan or curriculum, undergoing a background checks, and paying a licensing fee. Some locations might require you to acquire a childcare-specific license or permit, often necessitating additional requirements to be met such as first aid or CPR certification.

Zoning and Building Codes

Before you can operate a daycare from your home, you must ensure that your home is zoned properly. Some residential areas may not permit businesses to operate and others set strict controls on the number of children you can have in a residence. Navigating through this process may entail contacting your local zoning board or city hall to get your property inspected and approved. Along with this, you must also meet certain building code requirements. Your home will likely need to pass health and safety inspections looking at cleanliness, adequate space, emergency evacuation plans, safety features, and more.

Health and Safety Regulations

Home-based daycare providers are bound to certain health and safety regulations to protect children in care. This could include specific child-to-provider ratios, fire safety standards, hygiene protocols, proper fencing for outdoor play areas, safe storage for unpleasant substances etc. You may also need to provide proof of vaccination for any pets in the home and have health certificates for the children in your care.

Obtaining Necessary Insurance

Insurance is another critical legal requirement you need to meet before opening your home-based daycare. Business liability insurance can protect you in case of property damage, injuries happening on your property, or any kind of professional disputes. You should consult with an insurance agent with specific knowledge in home-based businesses or daycares to ensure you carry adequate coverage.

Contractual Agreements

Clearly drafted contractual agreements with parents are crucial to establish expectations, outline terms of service, and protect your business legally. This contract might contain information concerning your policies for payment, discipline, sick child protocol, and other pertinent situations. It's advisable to engage a lawyer while drafting or reviewing any contracts to ensure they observe contractual laws in your region.

Privacy Laws

As a daycare provider, you will be entrusted with sensitive information about children and their families. Understanding your legal obligations under privacy laws and maintaining the confidentiality of this information is essential.

Training and Certification

Certain regions require daycare providers to achieve particular training or certification such as CPR, First-Aid, and other childcare specific certifications. Ensure you meet these requirements before starting your operations.

3.2 Licensing Requirements

Licensing is a critical aspect when starting a home-based daycare business, as it ensures that facilities meet the necessary safety, care, and educational provisions required by law. These requirements often vary by state or country, so it is important to research and adhere to the specific regulations applicable in your area. However, general guidelines can be outlined to give you an idea of what to expect when seeking a daycare license for your home-based business.

Age and Education Requirements

Depending on the jurisdiction, there may be minimum age and educational requirements for home-based daycare providers. These requirements may include being a certain age (e.g. 18 or 21 years old) and possessing a high school diploma or equivalent. Some locations may even call for a college degree or childcare-specific certifications.

Background Checks

Security is a top concern for parents when leaving their children at a daycare facility. Licensing boards typically require comprehensive background checks for the daycare provider and any staff members involved in childcare. This generally includes criminal records, child abuse records, and any other relevant background information that may raise concerns about an individual's ability to properly care for children.

Licensing Training and Examinations

To qualify for a home-based daycare license, you and your staff may need to complete a specified amount of pre-licensing childcare training. This training could cover topics such as child development, health and safety, nutrition, business management, and discipline. In addition to training courses, some jurisdictions require daycare providers to pass a written examination to demonstrate their understanding of the material.

Health and Safety Regulations

Your home will need to meet specific health and safety requirements, as outlined by your area's childcare licensing board. These requirements might entail having a proper childproof home environment, implementing hygiene practices, having functioning smoke detectors and fire extinguishers, safe storage of hazardous materials, and properly fenced outdoor play areas. Regular inspections, either announced or unannounced, are often conducted to ensure ongoing compliance with health and safety regulations.

Provider-to-Child Ratio and Group Size

Licensing requirements almost universally include regulations regarding the provider-to-child ratio and group size. These provisions are intended to ensure that each child receives adequate attention and care in a safe environment. Ratios may vary according to the ages of the children being cared for, as infants and toddlers may need a higher amount of supervision than older children.

Enrichment and Curriculum

To meet licensing provisions, your home-based daycare may be required to implement a curriculum or planned activities that promote children's emotional, social, and cognitive development. Additionally, requirements may include the provision of age-appropriate learning activities, toys, and materials.

First Aid and CPR Certifications

Most jurisdictions require daycare providers and staff to obtain first aid and CPR certifications, ensuring individuals are equipped to handle medical emergencies that may arise while children are under their care.

3.3 Physical Space Requirements

One of the fundamental considerations when starting a home-based daycare is ensuring that your home meets the adequate physical space requirements necessary for the children's safety, comfort, and enjoyment. These can differ greatly depending on the regulations in your specific state or country, but the following points outline general requirements and considerations for preparing your space.

Adequate Space Per Child

There should be a specific minimum amount of indoor space dedicated per child in your care, often measured in square feet or meters. The square footage per child can vary based on the age of the child, local regulations, and whether the space will be used for active play, quiet activities, or sleep.

Outdoor Play Space

Outdoor play is an important part of a child's day and development. Regulations often require a certain amount of safe, fenced outdoor play space per child. This should be taken into account when assessing your property's suitability for a home-based daycare.

Safety Measures

Safety measures within your daycare space are a top priority. All hazards should be addressed including: sharp corners, stairs, uncovered outlets, or loose cords. All harmful substances and medicines should be locked away. All toys and equipment should be safe and age-appropriate. A secure fence is essential for an outdoor play area. Fire exits should be clearly marked and evacuation plans should be displayed.

Sleeping and Rest Areas

Depending on the ages of the children in your care and your operating hours, designated and comfortable sleeping or rest areas may be required. Each child might need their own separate crib, cot, or bed, all of which can take a considerable amount of space.

Bathrooms and Hygiene Facilities

Access to suitable bathroom and hygiene facilities is a must-have. These may need to be located on the same floor as the main daycare area and should be safe and appropriately sized for the children in your care.

Meals and Snack Areas

You will need to have a clean, safe area where meals and snacks can be prepared and served. Storage for food, whether it's a pantry, refrigerator, or cupboards, is significantly vital to consider. Also, dishwashing facilities are necessary to keep all utensils clean.

Activity and Learning Areas

Dedicated spaces for various activities and learning experiences are fundamental as well. This could include areas for arts and crafts, reading, active play, quiet activities, and more.

Accessibility

Ensure that your daycare is accessible. If you plan to include children with special needs or disabilities, you might need wider doorways, ramps, or other accommodations to make all areas of your home daycare easily accessible.

3.4 Safety Requirements

Safety is one of the primary concerns when operating a home-based daycare. To ensure the well-being of the children in your care, there are various safety regulations you'll need to meet. While local laws and guidelines may vary, here are fundamental safety requirements that are typically necessary when setting up and maintaining a secure home-based daycare.

Indoor Safety Measures

Indoor spaces should be free from hazards that could cause harm to children. The regulations would typically include:

- Secure all heavy furniture to the wall to prevent tipping.
- Safety gates at staircases and doorways should be sturdy and securely fastened.

- All electrical outlets should be covered with safety caps or self-closing outlet covers.
- Sharp corners and edges should be cushioned or covered.
- Small objects that could pose a choking hazard need to be kept out of children's reach.
- Ensure all high-risk chemicals, medications and cleaning supplies are secured in a locked cabinet.

Outdoor Safety Measures

Providing children with an outdoor play space is important, but it must be set up safely. This might mean:

- A sturdy fence around the play area.
- Regularly inspecting and maintaining outdoor play equipment to make sure it's in good condition.
- Ensuring the outdoor play area is free from poisonous plants, dangerous objects, and pests.
- Setting up shaded areas to provide protection from the sun.

Emergency Preparedness

Daycares must have a plan for emergencies, including:

- Ensuring smoke detectors and fire extinguishers are installed, accessible, and regularly maintained.
- Having clear evacuation plans in case of fire or other emergencies.
- Keeping a fully stocked first-aid kit, and all staff should be trained in first aid and CPR.
- Keeping all emergency contact information updated and accessible.

Hygienic Practices

Maintaining good hygiene is essential to prevent the spread of illness in a daycare setting. This might include:

- Setting up regular handwashing routines.
- Regularly cleaning and sanitizing toys, beds, tables, and other facilities.
- Ensuring nappy changing stations are adequately sanitized and disposed of properly.

- Ensuring food preparation and storage areas meet health and safety regulations.

Safe Sleeping Practices

For daycare providers who are caring for infants, it's essential to have safe sleeping practices, such as:

- Infants should always be put to sleep on their backs.
- Cribs should be free from pillows, stuffed animals, blankets, and bumpers.
- Babies should never be left unsupervised while asleep.

Supervision Requirements

Uninterrupted supervision is crucial to keep children safe:

- Daycare providers should always be aware and active in supervising the children in their care.
- Provider-to-child ratios set by local guidelines should be maintained at all times.

Chapter four

Important Skills and Qualifications

4.1 Necessary Educational Degrees/Certifications

Operating a home-based daycare requires unique qualifications and skills to ensure that children receive the highest level of care. While certain educational degrees or certifications may be necessary, specific personal qualities and skills also play a crucial role in maintaining a successful daycare.

Educational Degrees/Certifications

Some jurisdictions might require daycare providers to hold a high school diploma or equivalent, while others encourage or require a degree in early childhood education or a related field.

In addition to education, certifications in areas like First Aid, CPR, and Child Health and Safety are generally required. These certifications provide necessary skills for emergency situations and ensure that the daycare provider is prepared to deal with a range of health-related scenarios that may arise.

Other certifications might include Food Safety training, which can be extremely helpful in maintaining hygiene and safety standards when preparing and serving food to children. Furthermore, obtaining an early childhood education certification could be beneficial, as it demonstrates your knowledge of child development stages and educational activities appropriate for their age group.

Skills and Personal Qualities

Beyond education and certifications, certain skills and personal traits can prove to be invaluable for a daycare provider.

Patience

Working with young children requires an abundance of patience. Children often need guidance and repeated instructions, and may display challenging behaviors as they navigate their emotions.

Communication

Effective communication skills are crucial. A daycare provider must be able to communicate information about a child's day to parents, including what they ate, how they slept, and any significant behaviours or milestones.

Creativity

Creativity plays a vital role in developing engaging and educational activities that promote a child's growth and development.

Physical Stamina

Caring for children is physically demanding. The job often requires lifting or carrying children, bending or kneeling, and engaging in continuous active play.

Adaptability

Each child is unique, meaning childcare requires adaptability. A daycare provider must be capable of adjusting their approach based on a child's individual needs, preferences, and pace.

Organisation

Running a daycare not only involves caring for children but also administrative tasks such as maintaining records, managing finances, scheduling, meal planning, among others. Being organized will help ensure a smooth-running environment.

Leadership

It's important to foster a positive and respectful environment for children. A daycare provider needs leadership skills to guide children's behaviour in a constructive way.

4.2 Essential Personal Skills

While formal education and certifications undoubtedly play a critical role in setting up a successful home-based daycare, certain personal skills and traits can significantly improve the quality of care and experience you offer to the children and their parents. A successful daycare owner would typically exhibit a combination of the following key personal skills:

Emotional Intelligence

Understanding, recognizing, and managing both your emotions and those of the children in your care is a crucial aspect of running a daycare. Children learn from the emotional cues of the adults around them, so exhibiting strong emotional intelligence can help inculcate emotional stability in them. Emotional intelligence also helps in dealing effectively with the range of emotions you will encounter from both children and their parents.

Interpersonal Skills

Working with children and parents requires excellent interpersonal skills. This includes active listening, clear communication, compassion, and the ability to negotiate conflict. Fostering a warm, respectful, and understanding relationship with parents while maintaining open, candid communication is essential for successful daycare operations.

Problem-solving Skills

Children are unpredictable, and an ordinary day can present numerous small challenges that require quick thinking and problem solving. Whether it's mediating a disagreement between children or managing a sudden logistics issue, the ability to think on your feet and find immediate, effective solutions is a valuable skill.

Patience and Endurance

Children often need repeated instructions and guidance, and their high energy levels require constant attention. The ability to maintain calm and patience in both routine situations and during conflict or chaos is a must-have quality.

Observational Skills

Successful daycare providers are acute observers. By closely observing children's interactions and behaviours, they can identify potential development issues, understand individual needs, and create personalized learning experiences.

Creativity

Engaging young minds requires a creative approach. This might involve creating innovative educational activities, telling engaging stories, using interesting teaching aids, or even turning routine tasks into fun learning experiences.

Time Management

When handling multiple children with distinct needs and an array of administrative duties, effective time management is vital to keep the day running smoothly.

Passion for Learning

As a daycare provider, your role will not just be to supervise, but also to stimulate curiosity and learning in children. A genuine passion for learning and development can help create an environment that nurtures these values in children as well.

Chapter five

Creating a Business Plan

5.1 Defining Your Mission and Vision

Creating a robust business plan for your home-based daycare is an essential step before opening your doors to children. The foundation for this plan is your mission and vision statement. These statements outline your daycare's purpose (mission) and long-term goals (vision). They serve as a guiding force, helping you stay focused on your core purpose and aspirations. Here's how you can define the mission and vision for your home-based daycare.

Crafting Your Mission Statement

A mission statement explains the 'why' of your daycare business, the reason it exists. It will vary depending on your particular ethos towards childcare, your preferred approach, and the needs of the community you intend to serve.

A well-structured mission statement should feel clear, concise, and unique to your daycare. It should address:

- Who you serve (your target clientele)
- What you offer (your services)
- How you provide your services (your approach, methodology)

For example, a mission statement might look like this:

"To provide high-quality, affordable, and nurturing child care to our community's working parents. We aim to support children's growth and development in a warm, safe, and loving environment through play-based learning and creative activities."

Framing Your Vision Statement

Your vision statement offers a clear picture of what you aim to achieve in the long-term. It represents your daycare's aspirations and values - it's the 'north star' guiding your strategic planning.

A compelling vision statement should:

- Reflect the positive impact you aspire to have on the children and families you serve.
- Be ambitious, but also achievable.
- Inspire and provide direction to your actions and decisions.

An example of a vision statement might be:

"Our vision is to be the leading home-based daycare in our community, renowned for our commitment to holistic child-development, educational innovation, and strong collaboration with families. We strive for every child entrusted to our care to grow into curious, confident, and caring individuals."

5.2 Detailing Your Services

Your service offerings hold a central position in your daycare business plan. A comprehensive understanding and detailing of your services define your daycare's unique value proposition, influence your marketing strategy, pricing, and operations.

Types of Services

Home-based daycare services can typically include:

Regular Full-Time Care

This would involve providing a safe and nurturing environment for children throughout a typical working day, accompanied by activities designed to stimulate their development.

Part-Time or Flexible Care

Some families may require part-time or flexible daycare services. These could be parents with non-traditional work hours, or parents who work part-time and require childcare during specific hours of the day or week.

Before and After School Care

You could offer services to school-aged children by caring for them before and after school hours until their parents finish work.

Specialist Care

You may choose to offer specialist care that caters to children with special needs, infants, or older children who require more focused attention and care.

Elements to Detail

When detailing your services, consider the following elements:

1. Age Groups

   Specify the age bracket of children you will cater to. Parents should know if you offer services for infants, toddlers, pre-schoolers, or school-age kids.

2. Activities and Programs

   Detail the array of educational and recreational activities you offer. Include specific programs for physical activity, outdoor play, arts and crafts, music and movement, early literacy, or numeracy. Detail if you follow any specific childcare or educational philosophies in your curriculum

3. Health and Safety Measures

   Describe the safety measures, hygiene standards, and health practices followed at your daycare. This could include details of first-aid certifications, meal preparation, sanitation practices, and safety measures against COVID-19.

4. Staff Details

   Provide information about the staff, particularly their qualifications and experience in childcare.

5. Pick-up and Drop-off Flexibility

   If your service includes flexible pick-up and drop-off times, be sure to specify this. Some parents might be willing to pay more for this added flexibility.

6. Food Services

   Do you provide meals and snacks? If so, include details about your meal plans' nutritional content, accommodating food allergies, dietary restrictions, and your meal preparation methods.

5.3 Pricing Strategy

Pricing strategy is a fundamental aspect of your daycare business plan. Determining how much to charge for your services affects not only your revenue but also depicts the perceived value of your services. In setting your pricing, consider the balance between generating a profit and offering an affordable service that aligns with market rates.

To create an effective pricing strategy, consider the following:

Research Market Rates

Investigate the regional market price for daycare services, especially those with similar offerings as yours. Pricing yourself out of the market could lead to difficulty attracting clients. Conversely, setting fees too low may lead to potential clients questioning the quality of your service.

Calculate Operating Costs

The key to setting a profitable price is understanding your operating costs. This includes rent or mortgage (if relevant), utilities, meals, salaries, insurance, licensing, and any other maintenance costs. Knowing your expenses gives you an understanding of the minimum price you must charge to cover costs and benefit from a profit margin.

Value of Services

Assess the value and benefits that your daycare provides. If you offer unique or specialist services that enhance a child's experience and development beyond basic care, this can justify a higher fee.

Consider Different Fee Structures

Adapt your pricing to various services or circumstances, if appropriate. For example, you might have different fees for full-time care, part-time care, or drop-in rates. Discounts for siblings or long-term contracts can also be considered.

Additional Costs

Factors such as extra-curricular activities, field trips, or special events may incur additional costs. Decide whether these will be included in the fees or charged separately.

Payment Policies

Establish clear payment policies, including when payments are due, late payment penalties, and any deposit or registration fees. Also consider your sick-day policy and whether you will offer any refunds or credits for days when children are absent.

Chapter six

Setting Up Your Space

6.1 Optimizing Your Space for Children

Setting up a home-based daycare involves transforming domestic spaces into lively, safe, and nurturing environments where children can play, learn, and grow. Effective space management and organization are essential for stimulating activity and maintaining harmonious operations. Here's how you can optimize your environment for a successful daycare setup.

Safety Considerations

First and foremost, your home should meet the necessary safety standards for a daycare facility.

- Baby-proofing: Install safety gates, corner protectors, cabinet locks, and cover electrical outlets.
- Limit access to potentially dangerous areas such as kitchens, garages, or staircases.
- Ensure the availability of smoke detectors, carbon monoxide detectors, and fire extinguishers.
- Offer a clean environment, free from dust, allergens, and mold.
- The exterior should have a safe play area, devoid of toxic plants or potential hazards.

Space Organization

Effective space utilization can stimulate learning, enable physical activity, and facilitate group interaction:

- Activity zones: Create designated areas for different activities – quiet reading space, art and craft corner, dramatic play area, building blocks section, etc.

- Space for movement: Ensure there's ample space for children to move freely, consider areas for indoor physical activities.

- Resting area: Quiet, comfortable sleeping arrangements are essential for nap time.

Educational Environment

The surroundings should enlighten, engage, and foster curiosity among children.

- Educational resources: Make books, educational toys, and learning materials accessible.

- Display areas: Have designated spots to showcase children's artwork, projects or significant learning achievements.

- Natural elements: Incorporate plants, natural light, and nature-based play resources to create a soothing environment.

Storage Solutions

Consider smart storage solutions to stow toys, craft supplies, and children's belongings neatly.

- Lower shelves: Use low shelves or baskets for toys and materials, allowing children to access and return items independently.
- Coats and Personal Items: Have hooks or cubbies at children's height for their coats, shoes, and bags.

Ambience

The overall ambiance of your daycare should be warm, welcoming, and child-friendly.

- Colours: Use vibrant yet calming colours. Children respond positively to a colourful environment.
- Cleanliness: Maintain high standards of cleanliness. A neat environment encourages children to respect and take care of their surroundings.

- Lighting: Ensure your space is well-lit, ideally with a lot of natural light. Good lighting promotes a positive mood and productivity.

6.2 Necessary Equipment and Supplies

Equipping your daycare adequately is crucial for providing a comprehensive learning and growth environment. The types of equipment and supplies you need can range from essential safety installations to toys, educational materials, and furniture. Here's a comprehensive list of items you'd possibly need.

Safety Equipment

Your daycare must be a safe environment for children. Some safety measures include:

- Safety gates: These help in restricting children's access to certain areas.

- Outlet covers: To protect children from electrical shocks.
- Cabinet locks: For preventing children from accessing potentially dangerous contents.
- First-Aid Kits: Always keep stocked first-aid kits for managing minor injuries or emergencies.

Furniture

Daycare-specific furniture must be child-size, durable and safe, including:

- Tables and chairs: For eating, learning, and various activities.
- Sleeping cots: For rest time.
- Storage units: For organizing books, toys, craft materials, and personal belongings.

Learning and Play Materials

These materials provide the foundation for activities that stimulate emotional, intellectual, and physical development:

- Books: A variety of children's books, appropriate for different ages and reading levels.

- Art and craft supplies: Including non-toxic paints, brushes, child-safe scissors, glue, drawing paper, and craft materials.

- Educational Toys: Building blocks, puzzles, dolls, pretend play sets, motor skills toys, etc.

- Musical Instruments: Simple percussion instruments, xylophones, and musical toys can introduce children to the world of sound and rhythm.

Outdoor Play Equipment

If you have outdoor space, consider equipping it with:

- Play Structures: Slides, swing sets, climbing frames, subject to available space and safety considerations.

- Outdoor Toys: Balls, frisbees, tricycles, sandbox, gardening tools for children, etc.

Hygiene Supplies

Maintaining a clean environment is essential, especially considering younger children's habit of exploring with their mouths:

- Cleaning Supplies: Child-friendly detergents, disinfectants, paper towels, and other necessary cleaning materials.
- Personal Hygiene Items: Hand sanitizers, hand soaps, tissues, baby wipes, and toilet paper.

Food Service Equipment

If you'll be providing meals, you'll need:

- Child-Safe Cutlery and Dishes: Plastic or stainless-steel utensils and plates, sippy cups, etc.
- High Chairs: Depending on the age-group of kids, high chairs may be a necessity.
- Refrigerator: To store perishable goods if you will be preparing meals.
- Microwave: For quickly heating food.

6.3 Creating Safe and Engaging Play Areas

Designing engaging and safe play areas for children is integral to the success of a home-based daycare. Play areas must simultaneously fulfill several purposes: promoting physical activity, encouraging socialization, stimulating creativity, and ensuring children's safety. Here are practical guidelines to help you create safe, inviting, and enriching play spaces in your daycare.

Indoor Play Areas

Indoor play areas are essential for a variety of reasons, including adverse weather, structured learning, and physical movement. Create engaging indoor play spaces by incorporating:

1. Activity Zones: Dedicate separate areas for different forms of play, such as a reading corner, art station, and dramatic play area. This allows for

diverse experiences that contribute to children's overall development.

2. Safety Features: In addition to the standard safety measures of any daycare, pay special attention to soft flooring (such as interlocking foam mats) and ample space for children to move around safely.

3. Age-Appropriate Toys: Provide a mix of age-appropriate toys and games for various developmental levels. Ensure that toys are kept in good condition and regularly cleaned.

4. Storage: Use smart storage solutions (like labeled bins on low shelves) to keep materials accessible and organized. Encourage children to practice responsibility by returning items after use.

Outdoor Play Areas

Outdoor play areas provide opportunities for children to engage in physical activity, nature exploration, and fresh-air exposure while fostering motor skills development.

1. Enclosed Space: Ensure the outdoor area is secured with child-proof fences or barriers to maintain the children's safety.

2. Play Equipment: Incorporate age-appropriate and safe play structures like slides, swings, and climbing frames. Ensure these are routinely checked for damage or wear.

3. Natural Elements: Encourage nature-based activities by including plants, sand play areas, or bug exploration options. Include shade where possible to protect against sun exposure.

4. Surface Material: Use child-safe surface materials such as rubber mats or mulch to minimize injury risks from falls.

diverse experiences that contribute to children's overall development.

2. Safety Features: In addition to the standard safety measures of any daycare, pay special attention to soft flooring (such as interlocking foam mats) and ample space for children to move around safely.

3. Age-Appropriate Toys: Provide a mix of age-appropriate toys and games for various developmental levels. Ensure that toys are kept in good condition and regularly cleaned.

4. Storage: Use smart storage solutions (like labeled bins on low shelves) to keep materials accessible and organized. Encourage children to practice responsibility by returning items after use.

Outdoor Play Areas

Outdoor play areas provide opportunities for children to engage in physical activity, nature exploration, and fresh-air exposure while fostering motor skills development.

1. Enclosed Space: Ensure the outdoor area is secured with child-proof fences or barriers to maintain the children's safety.

2. Play Equipment: Incorporate age-appropriate and safe play structures like slides, swings, and climbing frames. Ensure these are routinely checked for damage or wear.

3. Natural Elements: Encourage nature-based activities by including plants, sand play areas, or bug exploration options. Include shade where possible to protect against sun exposure.

4. Surface Material: Use child-safe surface materials such as rubber mats or mulch to minimize injury risks from falls.

Multi-Age Play Areas

If you will be caring for children of varying age groups, consider how to adapt your play areas to accommodate differing needs and development stages:

1. Division: Separate play areas for different age groups. This can help prevent accidents and minimize conflicts between older and younger children.

2. Age-Appropriate Toys: Provide toys and materials suitable for each age group, ensuring they are engaging and developmentally appropriate.

3. Supervision: Remember that children of various ages require different levels of supervision during playtime. Ensure adequate supervision is provided at all times.

Chapter seven

Health and Safety Guidelines

7.1 Health and Safety Guidelines

While everyone hopes for the best possible day, unexpected incidents can occur in any childcare setting. One of the best ways to equip yourself for such emergencies is by undertaking First Aid and CPR training. This is not just recommended but often a mandatory requirement for home-based daycare providers. Here's an overview of how this training contributes to health and safety guidelines in home-based daycare.

Importance of First Aid Training

First Aid enables caregivers to respond effectively during a medical emergency. This could include minor incidents like cuts, bruises, minor burns, or more serious situations like choking, seizures, or allergic reactions. Adequate training gives providers the confidence and competency to handle these scenarios, potentially preventing them from escalating into more severe situations.

Key areas daycare providers learn include:

- Basic First Aid Techniques: Such as treating wounds, burns, bites, sprains, and managing situations like poisoning or choking.

- Recognition of Symptoms: Allows early intervention in case a child is displaying signs of illness.

- Handling Medical Emergencies: Equip providers with skills to address severe situations such as seizures or severe allergic reactions.

Importance of CPR Training

CPR (Cardiopulmonary Resuscitation) training is essential for every caregiver. It is a lifesaving technique used during emergencies when a child's heartbeat or breathing has stopped. Some situations where CPR may be required include drowning and suffocation, choking, or sudden cardiac arrest.

CPR training usually focuses on:

- Techniques for different age groups: CPR for infants and toddlers differs significantly from adults. A well-rounded CPR training will teach appropriate techniques for different age groups.
- Procedures: Providers will learn the sequence of actions to be taken.
- Use of an Automated External Defibrillator (AED): If available, using an AED can greatly enhance

chances of recovery and is typically included as part of CPR training.

Certification

In many regions, certification in both first aid and CPR is necessary to run a home-based daycare. This certification is typically valid for a specific period (commonly two years), after which renewal is required. It is advisable for all staff members to undergo this training for a multi-faceted safety approach.

7.2 Health and Safety Procedures

The maintenance of a robust health and safety regimen is an indispensable part of home-based daycare operations. These procedures serve not only to protect the children in your care but are also key to creating a professional and trustworthy childcare environment. Here are foundational health and safety procedures to consider:

Common Health Procedures

- Staff Immunizations: Ensuring all staff are up-to-date with immunizations can prevent the spread of illness.

- Child Health Records: Maintain up-to-date health information for each child, including allergies, dietary restrictions, and emergency contacts. Request parents to provide immunization records and regular health updates.

- Illness Policy: Develop a clear policy of how to handle a child's illness. Include guidelines on when a child should stay home, when they can return, and under what circumstances parents will be contacted.

- Medication Administration: Have a written policy on administering medication. This includes consent forms, dosage records, and specific storage requirements for different types of medication.

Hygiene Procedures

1. Hand Hygiene: Teach and enforce proper handwashing routines for staff and children. Supply hand sanitizers in strategically placed spots.

2. Routine Cleaning: Regularly clean toys, utensils, sleeping cots, and other surfaces frequently touched by children. Use safe, child-friendly cleaning supplies.

3. Toilet/Diapering Hygiene: Have specific routines for diapering and toilet activities, including washing hands before and afterwards, and properly disposing of soiled diapers.

Safety Procedures

- Emergency Evacuation Plan: Develop a clear plan/regimen for exiting the property in case of emergencies like fire, flood, gas leak etc. Practice these drills regularly with the children.

- Child Pickup Policy: Only authorized individuals should collect children. Ensure you have a system to verify this information.

- Injury Response: Develop a clear action plan for addressing injuries, which should include parent contact, report writing, and follow-up.

- Child Abuse Recognition and Reporting Procedures: Stay current with laws about reporting suspected child abuse—know the signs and whom to report it to.

Nutrition

1. Food Allergies: Keep track of any food allergies among children and ensure meals are planned accordingly to avoid an allergic reaction.

2. Safe Food Handling: Food safety should be a high priority, follow proper storage, preparation, and serving guidelines.

3. Balanced Meals and Snacks: Provide nutritionally balanced meals to ensure children's well-being and promote healthy eating habits.

7.3 Meals and Snacks Guidelines

Providing healthy and balanced meals and snacks to the children in a home-based daycare is crucial both to their well-being and overall growth. By devising a comprehensive and thoughtful food program, you not only support a child's physical and mental development but also promote good eating habits that can last a lifetime. Here is a guide to creating a nutritious meal plan that adheres to health and safety guidelines:

Planning Nutritious Meals and Snacks

- Balanced Approach: Aim to include food from all five food groups (fruits, vegetables, grains, protein, and dairy) while maintaining age-appropriate serving sizes.

- Age-Appropriate Nutrition: Different age groups have varied nutritional requirements. Plan your meal program accordingly (e.g., younger children require smaller, more frequent meals).

- Inclusivity: Be considerate of children with special dietary needs, food allergies, or cultural sensitivities. Ensure that your meal plans incorporate options that cater to these children.

- Variety: Introduce new and diverse food items regularly to broaden children's palates and help them explore novel flavours and textures.

Health and Safety Guidelines for Meals and Snacks

1. Food Allergies: Maintain thorough records of each child's allergies or intolerances. Ensure that meals and shared spaces are allergen-free zones to avoid cross-contamination.

2. Safe Food Storage: Properly store food items by following guidelines for temperature and container usage to prevent spoilage or contamination.

3. Safe Food Preparation: Follow food safety principles during meal preparation, such as washing hands, using separate cutting boards for different food items, and cooking at appropriate temperatures.

4. Hygiene: Practice and teach proper handwashing routines before and after meals. Encourage children to do the same.

Encouraging Healthy Eating Habits

1. Appealing Presentation: Make meals colourful and visually appealing to spark children's interest in healthy eating.

2. Role Modeling: Caregivers can set examples by exhibiting healthy eating habits themselves and eating together with children during meal times, emphasizing the benefits of balanced nutrition.

3. Education: Provide age-appropriate information about food groups, sources of nutrients, and the importance of healthy eating to children, encouraging curiosity about the food they consume.

4. Involving Children: Invite children to participate in simple meal preparation tasks or even help grow a garden. This encourages a meaningful connection with various food types.

Chapter eight

Developing Curriculum and Daily Activities

8.1 Creating a Child-Centered Curriculum

A well-structured curriculum is the linchpin of any successful daycare environment. Emphasizing a child-focused curriculum, one that delineates age-appropriate activities tailored to individual interests and developmental levels, can enrich a child's daycare experience and promote holistic growth. Here are some key guidelines for creating a child-centred curriculum for your home-based daycare:

Understanding Developmental Milestones

Identify the key developmental milestones for each age group to understand what skills children should be developing. Modify your curriculum to target these milestones, catering to a variety of developmental areas, including cognitive, emotional, social, and physical growth.

Child-Centred Curriculum Components

1. Play-Based Learning: Leveraging play as a potent medium for learning helps children absorb and process new information more effectively. Structured and unstructured playtimes promote problem-solving skills, creativity, and social interaction.

2. Language Development: Incorporate activities that improve communication skills such as reading storytelling, rhymes, and singing songs.

3. STEM: Engage children in simple Science, Technology, Engineering, and Mathematics (STEM) activities tailored to their age that stimulate their curiosity and logical reasoning.

4. Arts and Crafts: Craft activities foster creativity, fine motor skills, and self-expression.

Individualised Planning

1. Personalise Learning: Recognize each child's individual learning style, interest, and pace while planning activities. This ensures children remain engaged and see learning as a rewarding experience.

2. Observation and Documentation: Regularly observe and document children's interests, skills, and challenges. This information can guide you in updating and refining your curriculum.

Incorporating Routines

Creating routines, including transitions such as mealtime, nap time, or cleanup time, helps children understand time management, responsibility, and the concept of sequence.

Collaborating with families

Building a strong relationship with families can help create a holistic developmental plan. Sharing regular updates regarding a child's progress and involving parents in some activities can foster a stronger learning community.

8.2 Organizing Daily Activities

Organizing and scheduling daily activities is an essential aspect of managing a home-based daycare. Efficient planning ensures that children experience a comprehensive array of engaging activities, which, in turn, promotes holistic development. Here is a comprehensive guide to help you organize daily activities for your daycare curriculum:

Establishing a Daily Schedule

1. Structure and Flexibility: Create a schedule that offers consistency but leaves room for adjustments based on individual needs and any unexpected circumstances.

2. Balance: Ensure the schedule includes an assortment of activities that cover different areas of development—cognitive, physical, emotional, and social.

3. Age-Appropriate Timing: Arrange activities in ways that cater to the attention span and energy levels of different age groups. For example, younger children may require more frequent transitions between

activities, while older children can sustain focus for longer durations.

4. Routines and Transitions: Build in sufficient time for routines (e.g., meals, naps, and bathroom breaks) and smooth transitions between activities. Young children can become unsettled when rushed through transitions, so account for this time when planning.

Activity Selection

1. Variety: Include a myriad of activities that engage various learning styles and preferences. This may encompass play-based learning, storytelling, arts and crafts, outdoor activities, and group games.

2. Child-Centered Focus: Select activities that align with the children's interests, cultural backgrounds, and levels of development. By making activities

relevant and engaging, children find the learning process enjoyable and rewarding.

3. Incorporating STEM: Integrate age-appropriate STEM (Science, Technology, Engineering, and Mathematics) concepts into daily activities to foster curiosity, critical thinking, and problem-solving skills.

4. Social Skills Development: Encourage children to practice social skills through activities involving group interactions, such as collaborative art projects, games, or dramatic play.

5. Outdoor Time: Ensure children have daily opportunities for outdoor activities that encourage physical exercise, exploration, and connection to nature.

Adapting to Individual Needs

1. Differentiation: Be prepared to adjust planned activities to accommodate diverse learning styles, skill levels, and needs among the children. This may involve breaking activities into smaller steps, scaffolding the learning process, or providing additional support.

2. Observation and Feedback: Routinely observe children during activities and collect feedback to assess the success of your daily plans. Share these observational insights with parents to keep them informed of their child's progress.

8.3 Inclusion Strategies

Inclusivity is a cornerstone of any educational setting and even more poignant within a home-based daycare's intimate environment. Building an inclusive curriculum supports all children regardless of their abilities, cultural backgrounds, or special needs. Here are some essential guidelines for developing inclusive curriculum and daily activities:

Recognizing Diversity

Understand that children come from different cultural backgrounds, learn at different rates, and have unique strengths and challenges. By acknowledging this diversity, you can better tailor your curriculum and activities to accommodate all children.

Creating an Inclusive Environment

1. Physical Accessibility: Ensure the daycare space is safe, comfortable, and accessible to all children. For children with physical disabilities, adapt the environment as required, e.g., ramps, wide doorways, or tactile learning aids.

2. Sensory Considerations: Incorporate 'quiet zones' or 'sensory corners' for children who might need a break from sensory-filled activities. Utilize textured materials, soft lighting, relaxing music, or calming visuals to create a soothing space.

3. Cultural Representation: Decorate the daycare with materials reflecting various cultures. Books, posters, toys, and music from different cultures can foster an appreciation for diversity.

Adapting Curriculum and Activities

- Differentiated Instruction: Modify teaching strategies to meet individual learning styles, abilities, and interests. Break tasks into smaller, manageable steps; offer multiple ways to engage with materials, or provide additional support as required.

- Universal Design for Learning (UDL): Implement UDL principles for activity design, offering multiple means of engagement, representation, and expression to accommodate children's unique ways of learning.

Collaborating with Families and Specialists

1. Parent Partnership: Encourage parents to share insights about their child's unique needs, concerns, and interests. Incorporate their input into the curriculum and activity planning to ensure every child feels valued and included.

2. Specialists Involvement: Collaborate with specialists such as speech therapists, physical therapists, or special education teachers to create individualized plans for children with special needs.

Encouraging Social Inclusion

1. Group Activities: Facilitate activities that encourage interaction amongst children, fostering friendships, empathy, and understanding of differences.

2. Role-Play and Stories: Utilize role-play or storytelling to teach children about diversity, empathy, and acceptance towards others with different abilities or backgrounds.

Conclusion

Running a home-based daycare can be a gratifying and profitable venture. It's an opportunity to make a meaningful impact on children's lives and play a vital role in their developmental journey. However, establishing a safe, engaging, and profitable home-based daycare business involves a range of challenges and responsibilities.

Firstly, the cornerstone to a successful daycare is a child-centred curriculum that encourages holistic development. This involves designing activities centred around key developmental milestones, fostering both structured and unstructured play, engaging children in age-appropriate STEM activities, and incorporating routines that provide structure and predictability.

Secondly, organizing daily activities is crucial for a smooth-running facility. The secret to this lies in striking a balance between structure and flexibility while ensuring diverse, age-appropriate activities that cover various developmental areas. Adaptation according to individual needs, careful observation, and communication with parents are the keys to individualized planning.

Thirdly, inclusivity forms the bedrock of any effective child-care facility. By acknowledging and valuing diversity, we enrich our learning community and ensure that each child feels valued and included. To achieve this goal, home-based daycare owners can utilize strategies like differentiated instruction, creating an inclusive physical environment, employing Universal Design for Learning principles, and promoting social inclusion.

Moreover, navigating the financial landscape of the daycare business—pricing services competitively, managing expenses, and retaining profitability—is a key element of sustainability. Additionally, ensuring safety by creating a secure physical environment and following robust health practices is vital to gain parents' trust and building a reputable business.

Finally, fostering a strong relationship with families and collaborating with them to further children's developmental journey cannot be overstated. This creates a supportive and nurturing community fostering each child's growth and development.

From understanding developmental milestones to creating an inclusive environment, every step you take as a home-based daycare owner impacts a child's life. With prudent planning, dedication, and a passion for early childhood education, you can start and run a safe and profitable childcare business that enriches young lives, provides critical support to families, and flourishes as a respected venture.